EDDIE THOMPSON

Poetrylite

❦

Verses about life

with drawings by Peter Osborne

EDDIE THOMPSON

Poetrylite

Verses about life

with drawings by Peter Osborne

MEREO
Cirencester

Mereo Books

1A The Wool Market Dyer Street Cirencester Gloucestershire GL7 2PR
An imprint of Memoirs Publishing www.mereobooks.com

Poetry Lite: 978-1-86151-626-8

First published in Great Britain in 2016
by Mereo Books, an imprint of Memoirs Publishing

Copyright ©2016

Eddie Thompson has asserted his Right under the Copyright Designs and Patents Act 1988 to be identified as the author of this work.

This book is a work of fiction and except in the case of historical fact any resemblance to actual persons living or dead is purely coincidental.

A CIP catalogue record for this book is available from the British Library.

This book is sold subject to the condition that it shall not by way of trade or otherwise be lent, resold, hired out or otherwise circulated without the publisher's prior consent in any form of binding or cover, other than that in which it is published and without a similar condition, including this condition being imposed on the subsequent purchaser.

The address for Memoirs Publishing Group Limited can be found at
www.memoirspublishing.com

The Memoirs Publishing Group Ltd Reg. No. 7834348

The Memoirs Publishing Group supports both The Forest Stewardship Council® (FSC®) and the PEFC® leading international forest-certification organisations. Our books carrying both the FSC label and the PEFC® and are printed on FSC®-certified paper. FSC® is the only forest-certification scheme supported by the leading environmental organisations including Greenpeace. Our paper procurement policy can be found at
www.memoirspublishing.com/environment

Typeset in 9/15pt Bembo
by Wiltshire Associates Publisher Services Ltd. Printed and bound in Great Britain by Printondemand-Worldwide, Peterborough PE2 6XD

DEDICATION

To Enid
(En as in Endear - Welsh!)
On my meat you are the mustard,
On my sweet you are the custard,
On my egg you are the salt,
In the keg your are the malt,
To my fork you are the knife,
I thank my God you are my wife.

ABOUT THE AUTHOR

Eddie Thompson is an expatriate Manxman who settled in Milton Keynes with his Welsh wife Enid and daughters Kirsty and Gill in 1981. His verses are based on his experiences, observations and thoughts, hence (he says) their brevity; they cover a variety of subjects from Manx cats to Milton Keynes. Although Eddie has been versifying for many years, this is the first time any of his verses have been published.

Peter Osborne writes: "I love to put aside my oils and palette and join my friend Eddie Thompson, the wordsmith, poet and sideswiper, and add a few visuals to his verbals."

CONTENTS

Short ones

Limericks

Six-liners

Long ones

Longer ones

SHORT ONES

Move over William McGonagall, all is forgiven
For with howlers unheard of these verses are riven.

On Being Brief
That's Life
A Life of Rhyme?
The truth: discuss
My Psychological Crutch
The Ultimate test
We have a Plumbing Problem
What's his name again?
The Plotted Pant
Hanging On
The Harbinger of Summer
The Selection Process
Green Energy?
The Bird Bath
Celia Celia 2
Write Out 100 times
Mozart's Mass in C
What's your Beef?
Minimalism

ON BEING BRIEF

These verses are short – Christmas cracker length,
And it may be said with confidence, brevity is their strength,
They're my observations of life, laced with a sprinkling of jollity,
And it may be said with confidence, they're Christmas cracker quality.

THAT'S LIFE

In existential angst I wallow,
No longer fit for purpose,
An ageing piece of army surplus,
'Tis a bitter pill to swallow.

A LIFE OF RHYME?

The plan was, to record events and thoughts, record them all in rhyme
The problem is, there's not a lot of either, and I'm running out of time

THE TRUTH; DISCUSS*

As we're ground down in the mill of life,
Complete with its racks and pinions,
We may learn one philosophical gem,
There are no truths, only opinions.

MY PSYCHOLOGICAL CRUTCH

In a social situation,
I always talk too much,
In my plea for mitigation,
It's my psychological crutch.

This last line is a comment phoned in by a listener to the Jeremy Vine show (BBC Radio 2 11.1.12) during a discussion on the loss of the liner Costa Concordia, January 2012.

THE ULTIMATE TEST

Men, brace yourselves for the coming call,
Straighten your backs and prepare to walk tall,
The "Monstrous Regiment" will brook no stopping
So stiffen the sinews: we're going shopping,

WE HAVE A PLUMBING PROBLEM

My in-house waste-pipe overflows,
Which results in an almost hourly pee
The flow is free, the colour clear,
It's the frequency that's freaking me.

WHAT'S HIS NAME AGAIN?

We're watching a terrific tenor on telly,
Is he Welsh or Italian, this Andrea Pwllheli?

THE PLOTTED PANT

That's it, we'll buy Rosie and Noel a planted pot,
No no, hang on, a panted plot,
Sorry, sorry, I mean a plotted pont,
For goodness sake! It's a PLOTTED PANT.

HANGING ON

Before you start pointing the finger,
Yes, there are notes upon which I will linger,
Because when I catch a note I know,
I'm extremely reluctant to let it go.

THE HARBINGER OF SUMMER

Summer has come,

Throw open your shutters,

I've just heard the first hum,

Of the Council's grass cutters.

THE SELECTION PROCESS

She may be a ravishing beauty, a paragon, a jewel,

But does she understand the LBW rule?

GREEN ENERGY?

'Jesus wants me for a sunbeam'

Spreading warmth and light,

But I'm hoping for a better offer from British Nuclear Fuels.

THE BIRD BATH

Complete with soap and towel, song birds come and queue,

At the bird-bath in our back garden, where they make it a bit of a do

But there's always a party-pooper (in this case a feral pigeon) who,

Much to the others' annoyance, stands in the bath to poo.

CELIA CELIA (2)

To think of you with nothing on,

Is what I do all day long

From one hope I'll never stray,

I hope to see you thus one day.

Inspired by that lovely little poem 'Celia Celia' by Adrian Mitchell (1932-2008).

WRITE OUT 100 TIMES

I must not waste precious time,
Writing out couplets that rhyme.

MOZART'S MASS IN C

To those around me this is more than alarming,
For my struggle to sing it is a sort of self-harming.

WHAT'S YOUR BEEF?

We thought we were eating beef
From an unimpeachable source,
Can you imagine our grief,
When we were told it was horse?

MINIMALISM

'Tis my belief,
We should be brief,
So here my friends,
My message ends.

LIMERICKS

Limericks are meant to be frivolous,
Barrack room bawdy, not timorous,
The best are read on toilet walls,
They're rarely read in marble halls,
So let's hear it for limericks lascivious.

The Other Side?
Milton Keynes (2)
MCPs
Sleepless in Betws
Birds
A Helical Lexical
Hurdles
Enid's New Hip

THE OTHER SIDE?

How will I communicate, will there be a guide?
On whose table should I rap, from the other side?
Can there be such a place?
Is there really such a space?
Or is it all a hoax, are we taken for a ride?

MILTON KEYNES (2)

Milton Keynes, this amazing maze,
This criss-cross pattern of Streets and Ways
Of roundabouts
And ins and outs,
In my opinion, so worthy of praise.

It was once the joke of the nation,
Almost an obligation
To make fun of the place,
To kick sand in its face,
Now it's a favoured location.

I have this feeling, and I want to stress,
That it's just a feeling, no more, no less,
That this jaundiced view,
I attribute to,
The feeling that Brits don't like success.

MCPS

The Male Chauvinistic Pig,
Sees himself as Mister Big,
His superior attitude,
And absence of gratitude,
Secures his status as a despicable prig.

SLEEPLESS IN BETWS

The Noise! The Noise! It never fails
To steal my sleep and the wind from my sails,
It's four in the morning,
And another day dawning,
Whilst Enid sleeps, and snores for Wales.

BIRDS

Around our bird bath there was always a crush
Robins, wrens, the mistle thrush,
Et cetera et cetera,
There used to be a plethora,
Now we don't seem to see them much.

A HELICAL LEXICAL

Ergot, ergo, ego,
Ecto, echo, eco,
Words, words, words,
Have I joined the nerds?
Or am I just a freako?

HURDLES

There's always a hurdle to clear,
You clear one, then others appear
They take their toll
On body and soul
So what? GET OVER IT!

ENID'S NEW HIP

Let's hear it for Enid, 'Hip Hip Hooray!'
She's got a new hip and I earnestly pray,
That her leg spin's a corker
That she'll bowl a fine Yorker
And that with the new ball she's impossible to play.

SIX LINERS

Writing verse, of any kind,

Rigorously tests the mind,

Sadly mine but slowly grinds,

And tends to work with half-closed blinds

Operating 'midst these confines,

Limits me to just six lines.

Don't Disturb the Dust

Nowness

Accents

Just a Smile?

Manx Wallabies

Ageing (4)

Cynics

Oh No!

Future Imperfect

Don't tell the Neighbours Yet

The Wartime Role of Paper

Life's Mission?

Ethics

Mirror Mirror on the Wall

Handel's *Dixit Dominus*

Gnosis

Invisible?

Dies Irae

Fulfilment

Sounds Familiar

On the Wordsmith's Anvil

Lorraine's Recovery

Vic Brennan

Richard Caradog Evans (1913-1996)

Synchronicity

Virgos

Sing!

Stepping Outside

To not so boldly go

Therapy

Give me a 'Yes'

The Stuff of Dreams

Prompts

Nothing's simple any more

Rare Birds

On being recycled

Who will come a-wombling?

Problems, problems

A "Kebab" Poem

Speech as Song

Subjectivity

The Point of Poetry

The Ultimate Prize

The Other Elixir of Life

Lavatorial Philosophy

DON'T DISTURB THE DUST

Yesterday it seemed a good idea,
(But then again we'd been drinking beer),
To record my youth in verse,
Today I can't think of anything worse,
OK, to some it may seem worth a try,
But best, I think, to let sleeping dogs lie.

NOWNESS

With the future or the past, my mind is occupied,
The concept of the present something seems to override.
I've always had a problem with the here and now,
And need a Buddhist monk to somehow teach me how
To appreciate the nowness and to cultivate a sense,
That heightens my awareness of living in the present tense.

ACCENTS

What! All speak RP, that linguistic bleach?
And lose our patchwork quilt of speech?
No, accents matter, well, to me they do,
They act as a sort of spiritual glue,
They relate us to a particular place,
They're a link to our roots, our sacred space.

JUST A SMILE?

How good it is to cause someone to smile,
To help them to stop and pause awhile,
To lift their thoughts from the daily grind,
And just for a moment, help them unwind,
To know without doubt that you were the key,
That unlocked a good feeling, and set it free.

MANX WALLABIES

Wallabies on the Isle of Man? You're kidding me, right?
I kid you not; they are many and wild, an incredulous sight
In Oz I admit, it's no big deal,
Where they're big and furry with tourist appeal,
But the Isle of Man! That place to surprise never fails,
And how long will it be till they lose their tails?

AGEING (4)

It's no big deal, I suppose,
It's lasted well, heaven knows,
What I'm trying to say is, I've lost my mojo,
Signals to the engine room are always met with 'no go'
I'm sure doctor, that you've got it in one,
My get up and go has got up and gone.

CYNICS

Try to entertain a cynic,
It'll drive you to a mental clinic
No thanks, no praise, just criticism,
Plus the odd sarcastic witticism
They tend to be so overbearing,
Which makes their presence so despairing.

OH NO!

After an interjection, what do we usually find?
Yes, me too: I always did find grammar an excruciating grind,
Well, it's a word that expresses some sort of emotion,
Like 'blast' or 'blimey', something that shows a mental commotion,
Time's up, no points I'm afraid, you're clearly in the dark,
It's that comical cat's arse of punctuation, the exclamation mark.

FUTURE IMPERFECT

In ten years' time, what will be my lot?
What will I be like if I've lost the plot?
In a residential home for the old and the infirm
Alone, damp, smelly, spurned?
Will I molest lovely old ladies? Well, really, who can tell?
Oh my dear God, this is my idea of Hell.

DON'T TELL THE NEIGHBOURS YET

The disgrace, the shame, mother can't stop weeping
Personally I blame the company he's been keeping
And this higher education stuff, that must share the blame
For this gross humiliation, for dragging down the family's name
But there we are, it's his decision,
He wants to be a politician.

THE WARTIME ROLE OF PAPER

Mr Gell, demobbed, his face deadpan,
Told a story that did, well, astonish;
Toilet paper was scarce, so his story began,
And government sought any waste to abolish,
So the army issued two sheets per man,
One to wipe and one to polish.

LIFE'S MISSION?

So it's nature and nurture that set our life's course,
But perhaps we should look at an additional source,
And maybe this source is our life's mission,
To improve, by influence, another's condition,
A brief meeting, by chance, and then disengagement
Can lead to a life's complete rearrangement.

ETHICS

Ah yes, ethics, they're about being good,
The ethical life is behaving, more or less, as we should,
But being good isn't that simple, whys and wherefores abound,
And professors constantly argue over whether the theories are sound.
I don't think I'll bother being ethical, the theory I cannot digest,
I'll try to act out the practical, academics can keep the rest.

MIRROR MIRROR ON THE WALL

Mirror mirror on the wall,
The image I see does naught but appal,
The last time I looked,
I was visibly spooked,
For to me you reflected,
A body neglected.

HANDEL'S DIXIT DOMINUS

Handel's Dixit Dominus
Is a nightmare to sing, which is ominous,
It sorts the sheep from the goats,
If I sing it at all, I sing the wrong notes,
No amount of rehearsals will bring me up to scratch,
So I'll head for the door marked exit, and quietly lift the latch.

GNOSIS

I will not brook any criticism
Of those who pursue Gnosticism,
I know that it isn't, well, orthodox,
To the mainstream Christian it offers shocks
But I will not hold it a radical sin,
To believe that the Kingdom of God is within.

INVISIBLE?

Is it becoming increasingly apparent,
That to most you're invisible, or at least transparent?
That you're talked over, looked through,
And totally ignored by all but a few?
Then take heart and remember, like Brigadoon,
Your day will come, though it may not be soon.

DIES IRAE

Dear God, how will I be judged,
With all these blotted copybooks and all my others smudged?
I fear, with all my sins before me stabbing at my soul,
An eternity in purgatory, with no chance of parole.
Naked and alone, I will stand in "fear and trembling"
As you don your widow's cap and begin my disassembling.

FULFILMENT

Some twenty years or so ago,
Whilst looking for colonies of cowslips
I was, I remember, feeling flat,
There had to be more to life than that
But things have changed and though not a big hitter,
I have found my calling, I'm picking up litter.

SOUNDS FAMILIAR

The bleep was sharp, shrill, and right in my ear,
In a friend's kitchen, loud and clear.
'Did you hear that?' I asked of the host,
'My battery's gone flat, I'm as deaf as a post.'
'Not so my good friend, let your hearing-aid govern,
'Then you'll discover 'twas the microwave oven.'

ON THE WORDSMITH'S ANVIL

These are short ones; I only do short ones,
At least they're my own, not ready-made or bought ones,
They're straightforward, simple, nothing ever fraught ones,
Not the sort that needs much thought ones
They're neither strict nor polished, and far from being taut ones
I ought to stop, 'cos like I said, I only do short ones.

LORRAINE'S RECOVERY

Lorraine is recovering from a heart attack,
And after her op she'll soon be back
To her chirpy self with instructions to follow,
Which John will find hard to swallow.
There's one to drain the colour from his cheeks,
It's paragraph seven – no sex for six weeks.

VIC BRENNAN

Vic Brennan, whom I regard as a national treasure,
Whose very presence always brought pleasure,
To whatever he did he gave his all,
So now facing his maker, he can stand straight and tall
Truly, he was a gentleman, of that there is no doubt,
A magnificent example of what our lives should be about.

RICHARD CARADOG EVANS (1913-1996)

A quarryman, a gentleman, a closet intellectual,
Describe him in just six short lines? Totally ineffectual.
Richard Caradog Evans, of all things Welsh the essence,
How privileged we have been to have shared his very presence
Chapelgoer, kind and giving, unassuming writer,
His enquiring mind and humour made our lives a little brighter.

SYNCHRONICITY

You think it's coincidence? Don't you believe it,
There's something at work but we just can't perceive it,
It happens so often, defying the odds,
That we're left to believe it's down to the gods.
The phenomenon often brings us felicity,
It's described by Jung as 'Synchronicity'.

VIRGOS

Do you always tend to worry?
Are you always in a hurry?
Then you're a Virgo, I will wager,
For whom minor problems are mainly major
But please, take heart and misquote Descartes,
I worry, ergo I'm a Virgo.

SING!

Go on, just get out there and sing,
Close your eyes and give your voice wing,
Go for the feelings that singing can bring.
Sing for those you once held – and hold now – dear,
Sing for those that once gave – and give now – cheer
That's it, now quickly – wipe away the tear.

STEPPING OUTSIDE

We gradually learn what life is about
From knowledge learned by looking out,
Yet it's sometimes wise to step out of our skin,
And learn of ourselves by looking in.
"To see ourselves as others see us" and to be appalled,
To see our inflated egos, being badly mauled.

TO NOT SO BOLDLY GO

It's worrying, the effects upon the human race,
Of this lack of gravity they experience in space,
So many concerns, and none more so,
Than the restriction of blood to the lower torso.
To quote George Burns, how will men cope?
Sex will be like snooker played with a rope.

THERAPY

Apparently they're prone to depression,
Those who write poetry as a means of expression.
Should you know any poets who are melancholy,
Who seem to be going off their trolley,
Get them along to a poetry session,
Where they'll get a huge lift and indulge their obsession.

GIVE ME A 'YES'

It seems the word 'yes' is now out of favour,
Some have decided it's a word they can waiver,
The upwardly mobile will use, resolutely,
The grander, four-syllabled 'absolutely'.
Yet others use a word that could well impede,
Instead of plain 'yes', the affected 'indeed'.

THE STUFF OF DREAMS

Break out the Bristol Cream,
Raise your glasses on high,
Grease your gullet with Guinness,
Drink the Drambuie dry
Be upstanding, be happy, because
We have won the Ashes, in Oz.

PROMPTS

You may think that you're forgotten, of history bereft,
But there's always someone out there who's shared the path you've left,
Who can see your good and bad bits, and the dull bits in between
The bits you've long forgotten, by your memory unseen,
And by a strange coincidence, a face or voice will surface,
That stirs the soup of memory, maybe that's their purpose.

NOTHING'S SIMPLE ANY MORE

Swipe Card
Credit Card
Cash Card
Save & Spend
Club Card
Visa Card

Body oil
Conditioner
Shampoo
Shower Gel
Bath Oil

At the risk of sounding a grumpy old bore,
Nothing's simple any more
Options, choices, multiple facilities,
Technological wizardry, privatized utilities
Handbooks, manuals, instructions by the score,
I want to go on raging, "Nothing's simple any more!"

RARE BIRDS

Their sightings are becoming exceedingly rare,
We're told they're increasing, but honestly, where?
The last time I saw one - I mean in the wild,
Such a lovely sight, I stopped and smiled,
Ah, they've been rounded up, sedated, cemented,
In Sunnyridge Homes for the old and demented.

ON BEING RECYCLED

When you're up for recycling, what will you choose?
A wealthy tycoon on a permanent cruise?
The world's your oyster, so what's your choice?
An Italian tenor, with a fabulous voice?
Or an idle layabout, of no earthly use?
Well, you're getting close - I'd be a recluse.

WHO WILL COME A-WOMBLING?

Who will come a-wombling, a-wombling with me?
Picking up the litter' 'till our patch is litter free,
Shopping trolleys, broken brollies, shattered glass and plastic
Rubber tyres, electric fires, the situation's drastic.
We could RV at three on Sundays, by the butchered tree,
Who will come a-wombling, a-wombling with me?

PROBLEMS, PROBLEMS

Problems, troubles, worries and strife,
They all come under the heading LIFE,
There isn't a cure,
But one thing's for sure,
However impossible we think they get,
This time next year we'll have a different set.

A "KEBAB POEM" *

A kebab poem like this has a skewer running right down its middle,
Purists may see it as an impure form of poetry,
Many will shout 'Horse manure!' and suchlike insults,
And call them weak and poor, insecure, namby-pamby flim-flam
But hopefully some, fewer I know, will smile at the style.
Personally, I like its lure, it's different, that's for sure.

* 'Kebab Poems', mentioned on BBC Radio 4 'Front Row' 19.2.09

SPEECH AS SONG

Some phrases, more than others, have a certain swing,
Some phrases, moreover, encourage us to sing
Take, as an example, 'Me old brass jam pan',
(Which begs to chime with 'A Chinese sampan')
It's the rhythm, the stresses, the ups and the downs,
It's akin to singing; well, that's how it sounds.

SUBJECTIVITY

We're told we shouldn't surmise, we're told to be objective,
To be the scientific, empirical detective,
To be slow to believe and to avoid being credulous,
And to ignore our implanted personal prejudice.
But in spite of this advice and whatever else they say,
Subjectivity is sovereign, get over it, OK?

THE POINT OF POETRY

Well here we have it; it's out at last,
On the twenty-sixth inst. it appeared in The Times,
And to tell you the truth, it has left me aghast.
Purist poets may find this prickly,
But the point of all their dazzling rhymes,
Is to say a lot but to say it quickly.★

★ *Philip Collins in The Times, 26.11.08*

THE ULTIMATE PRIZE

It's a personal view,
But between me and you
The ultimate prize,
At least in my eyes
Is beyond my reach, and yours too I fear,
It's the unsullied conscience, the conscience clear

THE OTHER ELIXIR OF LIFE

For a failing libido or a good singing voice
I recommend my gargle of choice,
It's that Queen of Stouts, that confidence giver,
It's the life-giving waters of the Liffey River.
A pint of this 'Black Stuff' your ills will upend,
The elixir of life is Guinness, my friend.

LAVATORIAL PHILOSOPHY

A worrier, sitting on a toilet bowl,
Likened life to a toilet roll,
He'd stumbled on a well-known truth,
A truth that most of us know
That the nearer it gets to the end,
The quicker it seems to go.

LONG ONES

Fear not, take heart, and correct me if I'm wrong,
But nothing in this section is more than one page long.

Spinoza (1632-77)
The Meaning of Life (2)
Image
Doodling Again?
The Mosaic
The Wheel Turns
Overheard in Downton Abbey
The Tup
Life's a Bugger
Mail Call
Untitled
Ten Thousand Plastic People
Litter
Those mysterious transactions
The family tree
Oh Edward Bach
Ambition thwarted
Wakes
Conniburrow Observed

The Well of Forgetfulness
Is this the Way?
The Old Boy's Allergy
Old Comrades
Conniburrow Pond
Hats
Immoral Bards
Enthusiasm Please
Janet and Vic
National Poetry Day
Thompson
"Bring Something Lascivious"
"I'm Reviewing the Situation"
Eccentrics
Dear Madam
Advice
Cheerleading
Maidens
Jenny's Drones
The Fate of Poets

So why do I do it?
Cock Robin is Alive and Well
Accents (2)
Place
Life's Steeplechase
Hype
Keeping Calm
A Defence Mechanism
Welcome to Litter World
Breaking Wind in Chapel
Culture? Whose Culture?
The Visit
A Sort of Conversation
The Post
Red taped
Oh No! A Bass Entry
"And we shall be Changed"

SPINOZA (1632-77)

Benedict de Spinoza, now there's a name to savour,
And of all philosophical thoughts, his are the ones I favour
"God is Nature - Nature is God", it's an it, not a he, nor a she,
If that's good enough for Einstein, then it's good enough for me.
He's the precursor of the Green Movement, and Freudian analysis,
And saw our anthropomorphic gods as an intellectual paralysis
And as for free will, that old running sore,
No, our every act is determined by what has gone before.
His God doesn't set standards, and has no concern for man,
It neither loves nor hates, it doesn't judge or plan
Body and mind die together; there is no life eternal,
The union of mind with nature, that's the prize, the kernel
With organized beliefs his thoughts directly collided
Pantheist or Atheist? his critics are still divided.
Please, read his works, and if you find them, well, obtuse,
There are some good interpretations, so there's really no excuse.

THE MEANING OF LIFE (2)

"What do you think is the meaning of life?"
This question was thrust upon me by two young men,
Two well-mannered, well-dressed, confident young men,
American missionaries, offering salvation
To what they must see as a decadent nation.
For once in my life my reply was ready,
With a quote I've been nursing for twenty-five years
So I took off the safety catch and let them have both barrels:
"Life has no meaning other than that which we care to give it."
So we have but two choices, leave it or live it.
And walked on.

IMAGE

What you see is what you get,
That ain't necessarily so
What we see, I'm willing to bet,
Is a surface sheen, designed for show,
It's all down to the image makers,
Those mind-bending, elaborate fakers.

Image, imagine, imagination,
There is a definite link
An image can be a subtle temptation
That aims to affect the way that we think
So we have to get behind the veneer
For any substance to hopefully appear.

But I'm being cynical, there is an upside
For individuals with low self-esteem
Improving their image can instil a new pride,
A new view of self, a new head of steam
So I'll work on my body shape, cut down on the beers,
Sort out my wardrobe, defoliate my ears.

Amidst much anguish and family debate
My bright new positive image awaits.

DOODLING AGAIN?

I rarely write a mood rhyme, I really don't know how,
You rarely write a rude rhyme, really? Wow!
He rarely writes a crude rhyme, so he can take a bow,
She rarely writes a lewd rhyme, well, not now.
We rarely write a booed rhyme, as it always starts a row,
You rarely write a poo-pooed rhyme, because you're too highbrow
They rarely write an understood rhyme, meow, meow, meow.

THE MOSAIC

The Breakaway Kingdom of Cornwall,
The Central Coalition, (East and West Midlands),
The City State of London,
The East Anglian Alliance of Norfolk and Suffolk,
The Federation of East Coast Ports,
The Independent State of West Wessex,
The League of Home Counties,
The Northern Territories (Northumbria, Cumbria and Durham),
The Maritime Province of Merseyside,
The People's Democratic Republic of Sheffield,
The Sultanate of Luton and Leicester,
The Union of Lancashire, Cheshire and Greater Manchester,
England (what's left), capital York.

THE WHEEL TURNS

Dissidents, your time has come,
So raise your banner, beat your drum
For England is fragmenting, Home Rule is in the air,
Push your 'National Interests' to ensure you get your share
Be part of the mosaic of mini nation-states,
To compete with each other, and enter into dire straits.

OVERHEARD IN DOWNTON ABBEY

When Lady Mary said, "I'm going upstairs to remove my hat",
She was referring to something other than that
Likewise Carson's "I really must sound the gong";
If that's what you thought he meant, you were wrong.
They are euphemisms; they were off to the loo
But they couldn't say, 'I'm off for a poo'.
The Earl and Cora would have had a fit,
Had they heard someone say, 'I'm off for a ---- '.

THE TUP

What exactly is a tup? That may well be asked by city folk,
Possibly with caution, as they'd think it a joke
Well, it's a promiscuous ram, with the enviable ability
(Enviable that is, to young rams, yet to prove their virility)
To impregnate an entire herd
Awesome, maybe, could be the word.
The rest of the year he rests, building himself up
To do the same next year, when the call goes out for a tup
To some, that would have a certain appeal;
To me, it sounds like a pretty good deal.

LIFE'S A BUGGER

Life can be a bugger, but at least we're alive
What's the alternative? I can think of five.

Everlasting nothingness, a dark and timeless blank,
The bookies' odds-on favourite, the atheistic plank.

Purgatory: "A place of expiation, suffering or remorse."
That doesn't sound a ton of fun, not an option I'd endorse.

And then of course there's heaven, the ultimate reward,
But I've heard it said it's empty, you'd be permanently bored.

Or then again, to roast in hell, skewered on a spit,
Forever mind, eternity, in a dark satanic pit.

Or we could be recycled, that could well appeal,
But as what, a hamster, on an ever-turning wheel?

After weighing all the options, I prefer to survive.
Yes, life's a bugger, but let's be glad we're alive.

MAIL CALL

There was a time when letters came through the letterbox
Now a letter through the door blows off our cotton socks
With a letter on the mat, there's a minor commotion,
A suggestion of excitement, a flutter of emotion.
Back then, a letter from home was like manna from above,
A communication comparable to Noah and the dove
The messages they brought were good, but sometimes bad,

Like, 'The girl from the coal office has run off with your Dad
And to John, 'Your body with kisses one day I will cover',
Then later, 'Dear John I'm sorry, but I have found another'.
But it was a postal service that we could truly trust,
'The mail must get through', come what may, or bust,
So let us raise our glasses to the good old GPO,
And to its military cousin, the BFPO.

UNTITLED

He, she, or maybe they, are getting their `kicks' by having their fix
On a bench near here
That's bad enough, but their needles and stuff
Are left around, on the bench, on the ground.

It's more than the mere sight of it all,
It's the blight and pathetic plight of it all
It's the thought of a life in tatters,
A life in which just the fix matters.
They are lives that I fear we have failed,
Some, I'm sure, we've curtailed

But the genie is out of the jar,
And the damage it's doing,
The whole world is rueing
So what can we do to relight their star?

TEN THOUSAND 'PLASTIC PEOPLE'

As a fan of MK Dons I'm plastic,
So says hack Rick Broadbent, playing to the gallery,
Yet another 'clever' remark with which to earn his salary.
I sense that it's written in bile, it's definitely gastric
Ten thousand plastic people (that could be seen as artistic),
It's yet another insult, but I refuse to go ballistic.

Although the insult's barbed, it is but just the latest,
Of course it's his opinion; he's entitled to express it,
And he has the ear of many, to whom he can address it
And yet as insults go, it ranks amongst the greatest.
All hail his bitter wit?
Frankly, I don't give a shit.

Journalist Rick Broadbent's opinion of MK Don's fans in his column 'Couch Potato' in The Times, 6th August 2011.

EDDIE THOMPSON

LITTER

Undelivered newspapers dumped in wayside ditches
Umpteen plastic bottles on the lines of football pitches

Tin cans and rubbish, everywhere I look; I'm just at a loss,
It's the signature of people who couldn't give a toss

Someone's cherished motor-bike, stolen, dumped then torched,
Leaving underpasses black and tarmac pitted, scorched

Midst microwaves and mattresses, primroses still push through,
Should they ever stop, litter louts, that'll be down to you.

And those graffiti 'artists', I'll wager an odds-on guess,
They've never made a thing in their lives, except a bloody mess.

Education, say the councils, that's the path to take,
But the path is strewn with engine blocks, come on, for goodness sake!

We can't blame the councils, they're waging a constant fight
Against a mind-set intent on inflicting, an undesirable blight.

THOSE MYSTERIOUS TRANSACTIONS

When I was a boy, too long ago dammit,
On the Isle of Man, a different planet,
Danny the barber,
In Water Street, close to the harbour,
Would ask of his clients, when giving them change,
A question that struck me as interesting, strange
It was asked sort of secretly, almost slyly,
And the customer answered, "Yes please", shyly,
I thought it to do with the customer's hobby,
"Something for the weekend, Bobby?"

THE FAMILY TREE

"You must come and see the family tree.
It's big and fine - from an ancient line."
"Yes please" I reply, and stifle a sigh,
Because mine of course is like spindly gorse.

It was in the hall and covered a wall,
Selwyns and Dilwyns, Rhys, Prys and Heulwens
It's shown with a pride, whilst inside I hide
My thin shaky line, my vulnerable vine.

But no need for shame, it's only a game,
So then I thought, well, it's high time to tell
Of a gem I can flush from my family bush.
It's time to be proud and shout it out loud:

"My grandfather Dick, for a wife did pick,
It's just uncanny, grandmother Fanny."

(it's true!)

OH EDWARD BACH

Bach's B Minor Mass screws him up completely,
So he's giving it a miss, quietly, discreetly,
It's a mass too far and will stretch him fit to break,
He's sung it twice before, and always felt a fake.

Filling him with fear and trepidation, it brings on a rational dread,
For trying to sing it before brought headaches that put him in bed
It really is beyond him, so he'll take the easy way out,
And leave it to those who enjoy it, to watch the match with a stout.

AMBITION THWARTED

I would like to write a villanelle,
And try some concrete-poetry, that surely, must be fun,
Or cynghanedd, and haiku as well,
Or an acrostic, or list-poem, which this could well become.

You must be joking, you cannot be serious!
Sestinas and sonnets? No, you'll never hack it,
Avant garde poetry? You must be delirious,
Clerihews and limericks, that's your rhyming bracket.

WAKES

Wakes are not the time for solitary meditation
But for a life, a communal celebration
And throughout there's a thought that sets my flesh tingling
The deceased's spirit is amongst us and mingling
Aware that their final act on earth,
Has pulled people together with tears and mirth,
The great mystery to those gone is no more,
They've caught an earlier bus, and they know what lies in store
It's a thought.

CONNIBURROW OBSERVED

Why this sudden, welcome, interest in Conniburrow Estate?
Yes we have our problems, which I won't overstate,
But why now, and by whom, and will it improve our lot?
Is it an academic exercise, a degree course, or what?
Are they mature students, doing Human Geography?
Or maybe some sort of Urban Anthropology?
But to the observers I hope it has occurred,
That any observation affects the thing observed.

EDDIE THOMPSON

THE WELL OF FORGETFULNESS

So, we've been dipped in the Well of Forgetfulness,
We all have
Apparently it's a prerequisite for re-incarnation,
According to Hans Holzerl* that is.
Once on the 'other side' we're given a choice
By a sort of clerk - we can either stay there
Or have another go here,
So everyone on 'this side' has chosen to return,
(Life on the 'other side' can't be all that great then)
When one's number is called you are passed through the well
Sometimes the water doesn't quite touch everywhere,
And these dry spots are the cause of déja vu.
It's a neat explanation,
Unscientific and of course totally impossible to prove,
So it's a pipe dream to place amongst the many others
Concerning the Great Mystery.

'The Well of Forgetfulness'
It has an unforgettable ring about it, don't you think?

Hans Holzer, investigator of the paranormal, 1920-2009

IS THIS THE WAY?

To become a poet of literary measure
Possibly even a national treasure
Makes your verses impenetrably dense,
No matter their meaning doesn't make sense
Ensure your material
Is presented as ethereal
Lean heavily on the existential,
Reviewers will recognise great potential
Be obscure,
Leave your listeners insecure
Be licentious,
Brazen and pretentious
Die young in a foreign land
Be anything, but don't be bland.

THE OLD BOY'S ALLERGY

This is what Paul Phillipson said
Speaking from his hospital bed
"See that old boy over there?"
I sneaked a look, didn't stare,
"Yesterday he gave us a laugh
As he answered questions from hospital staff
He must have been feeling pretty dire,
When, 'Any allergies?' I heard one enquire,
The old boy, understanding not,
Stared and shouted loudly, 'What?'
'Is there anything you can't take?
It's simple enough for heaven's sake.'
Pens poised, they awaited his answers,
'Yes', he said, 'Ballet dancers'."

OLD COMRADES

Those once young cold war warriors, of what are they now dreaming?
Standing by their lethal chargers, steel tanks ready, gleaming?

Fangio Fisk, Kiwi Clements, Kipper Heron, Osram Light
Nobby Kennedy, Donkey Dick Fairclough, Chalky White.

Are they falling in 'crews front', with commanders on the right
Or crashing out midwinter, in the middle of the night?

Or in a Sennelager pub drinking Paderborner beer,
Or frozen stiff on Soltau, on a 'Cent' stuck in gear?

Or with half the British army, on the north German plain,
Ploughing up the landscape in the heavy autumn rain?

Of days corked up with Ginger Pud, long-term constipation,
And when at last the gates did flood, cat sanitation?

Of Oscar in the nick again, killing zones and griddle,
Or of the Regimental Police versus those on the fiddle?

Or marshalling hunter trials for officers on horses,
Of Padre's Hour, site guards or never-ending courses?

Fatigues in the cookhouse, compo - dodgy petrol cookers,
Or of fräuleins, without exception, fantastically good lookers?

Of the days when they had hair, and squaddie humour beaming
Those once young cold-war warriors, of what are they now dreaming?

CONNIBURROW POND

With Conniburrow Pond,
I'm forging a bond
A unique oasis,
In the strangest of places.
But some undesirables, determined to spoil it,
Are using the place as a public toilet.
As a lover of nature, I'm sorely offended,
It's the bottom line, no pun intended.

HATS

Not so long ago, or considerably less than that,
A man's class was revealed by the obvious height of his hat,
Tall top-hats were worn by the wealthy,
The gentry, the bigwigs, the financially healthy
Bosses and bankers wore bowlers, as did all the middle-classes,
Which placed them above the proletariat, the unrewarded masses.
Holding up this class-ridden structure, painfully aware of the gap,
Was the salt of the earth, the working man, wearing his flat cloth cap.

IMMORAL BARDS

When versifiers gather together,
It's only a matter of when, not whether,
Their verses lewd,
Carnal and crude,
Immoral, improper every word,
Alcohol fuelled, are going to be heard.

These verses are humorous
Bawdy and numerous
Making the sex act appear hilarious,
By describing positions physically precarious.
If portraying life, sex can't be excluded,
And they're enjoying describing sex denuded.

ENTHUSIASM PLEASE!

You were always, well, so enthusiastic,
Now it's as if you are made of plastic
Over many events you once enthused,

Now it's as if you've been excused.
It's to be expected, the experts tell us,
That the ageing process makes us less zealous,
But that's an unacceptable attitude,
A condescending crappy platitude.
It's an opinion that we should with vigour attack
And have it removed like dental plaque.
So get furious, angry, rant and rage,
Show them that passion doesn't die with age,
You'll know that something has lit your fuse,
It'll be something over which to enthuse.

JANET AND VIC

They're always in the West Stand, alongside the press, and
They'll be together at Stadium MK,
That is, at every home match, and
There, at half-time, we will meet for a five-minute chat
These five minutes are important to me as
They frame the time during which I shyly try to support them,
They are Janet and Vic, who are facing Vic's illness together, but
This five-minute meeting benefits me more than them as
Their positive views are a treat to hear and
They send me to the East Stand uplifted, even
Though we may be facing defeat
Thus the last visit, during the last home game of the season, was
Thought an opportunity to repay them with a chuckle and I gave
Them a copy of my silly scribbles.
They responded in kind in humorous verse and
This has gone into our family archive, with thanks,
They will be there next season,
Then we can shout together "Come on you Dons!"

NATIONAL POETRY DAY

Give three cheers, hip, hip, hooray,
Today is National Poetry Day
Dig out your favourite villanelle,
Your ditties, doggerel and limericks as well
Give air to your odes and romantic sonnets,
Don't hide your hobby under your bonnets
Voice your clerihews, couplets, serious free-verse,
Be brave ye bards, swear, cuss and curse
Recite your views on life, in all its totality
Rappers rap with passion and unrestrained vitality
Verses, doleful or brimful of mirth,
Today is the day to give them birth.

THOMPSON

"Surname?" I'm sometimes asked, not always politely,
"Thompson", I reply, not always brightly
After which will come the question, of this there's no doubt
"Is that Thompson with a 'p', or the Scottish way, without?"
To which I will answer, "I always have a 'p' in the middle",
(Do you get it? 'P' as in pee as in piddle).
This may raise a sardonic smile,
And 'clever dick' is entered, later, on my file.

Why can't I have a Manx name,
Like Kinvig, Mylchreest or Orry Quane?
But Thompson it'll have to be,
With its silent 'h' and silent 'p'
What's their purpose, why are they there?

They're completely redundant, totally spare
To any philologist this'll be a breeze,
So, answers on a postcard please.

"BRING SOMETHING LASCIVIOUS"

You've asked us to bring something lascivious,
A word about which I was completely oblivious
My dictionary defines it as 'exciting sexual desire'
Blimey! Maybe I could sing, "Come on baby light my fire",
Bring something, lewd crude and rude, something outrageous,
Well, forget the 'Zulu Warrior', I'm not that courageous.
"Come and perform your vice-ridden verses."
What? And reveal our wet-dreams of nymphomaniac nurses?
Okay, I'll see what I've got,
But of verses lascivious, there's not a lot.

For 'Poetry Kapow! (the Slam of Sins…) Wolverton.

"I'M REVIEWING THE SITUATION..."

All right, if you've got two minutes to spare, I'll tell you why I'm bitter,
It's because we're swamped with immigrants and ankle-deep in litter,
Plus, the pillars of our society are cracked and slowly crumbling,
And almost to a man, we're racked and woefully grumbling
Our politicians have been exposed as dishonest, devious and greedy
What hope does that offer, especially to the needy?
And when you're on the phone beware,
Big Brother's listening, so in what you say, take care
Incompetent greedy bankers have lost all their banks their cash,
This and the government's bail-out, ushered in a financial crash,
The police stitched up a cabinet minister,
Don't you find that spookily sinister?
The working class are demonized as 'chavs'
(Council Housed and Vulgar), by both the media and affluent 'haves'
The church's leadership had a nest of child molesters,
Is it any wonder there are riotous protesters?
The elderly in care homes have been physically abused,
Placed on a restricted diet and from a decent old-age excused
Our armed forces are being cut to the bone,
God help us if we have to stand alone
Scotland may soon be an independent nation,
This will be for the United Kingdom, a mutilation
Our senior football clubs are bought up by foreigners, filthy rich
And in Premier League games, there's rarely a Brit on the pitch
Show business seems to be brimming with drug devotees,
Who think they're beyond the law and try to do as they please
But hey ho, that's the way it is, so sing along with me,
A song we sang in Sunday school, or was it on our mother's knee?
"THERE IS A HAPPY LAND FAR FAR AWAY..."

ECCENTRICS

Eccentrics, it seems, have all but disappeared
It's more than strange, I think it's weird
When I was a lad we were blessed with so many
They really were ten a penny
So many in fact that it was hard to tell
What was the norm, where the line fell.
So why are their numbers falling?
Whatever the reason their loss is appalling
We need people who are unconventional,
Whose odd behaviour is unintentional
Who are off-centre in an amusing way,
With their innocence clearly on display.

So if an eccentric you know,
Let the relationship grow,
Though their behaviour be out of the box,
We need the difference, it'll fool the fox.

DEAR MADAM

You've turned me down again,
For reasons unknown - some faults that I own,
Your fifteenth rejection since - I don't know when.
I thought I'd a chance
With Exams Clerk, part time - well, I'm well past my prime,
And I'd hoped you say yes - not lead me a dance.
My name's a joke I'm sure.
"He must be thick - well, not very quick."
But my wish to be with you was perfectly pure.

I'm too old for you now.
It's not how you'll feel but you've lost on the deal.
If only we'd met, I'd have won you, I vow.
So, we're through you and I,
It's over at last – you're part of my past.
Thanks for your interest, good luck and good bye.
Never Yours
Eddie Thompson

My response to receiving my fifteenth rejection to job applications with the Open University, August '97

ADVICE

If you want to grab the reader's attention,
And then ensure their continued retention
Expand the truth to near invention,
Bring them into an added dimension.
This may entail reprehension,
Not to mention strong contention
Let this tension induce apprehension,
Stick to the rules, follow convention.
Would you believe it?
Would you Adam and Eve it?
Rules and tools, dos and clues, files on styles,
When my only aim is to raise some smiles.

CHEERLEADING

I'm drawing attention to the world of worriers,
And their fellow travellers, bad news couriers
To those who inhabit our default setting,
Who live amidst angst and constant fretting.

To those with foreheads deeply furrowed,
In whose trenches misery has intrusively burrowed
To harbingers of doom and gloom,
And those who moan from womb to tomb.

Of course life has a dark side, of that we're all aware,
Let us recognize those souls who are wasted walking there
Guide them somehow; shine your bright light,
Help them, please, to walk out of their night.

MAIDENS

Green takes strike and drives the first ball to mid-on; and there is no run,
He tickles White's next ball to fine-leg; and there is no run,
A good forward defensive stroke, fielded by the bowler; and there is no run
The ball pitches off the off-stump and is kneed away: and there is no run,
A full toss but Green is unable to get it away, and there is no run,
The last ball of the over is pulled to short mid-wicket; and there is no run.
Brown now faces Black and flicks the ball to cover-point; and there is no run
A good looking stroke to backward-point: and there is no run,
Brown slices this delivery off the face of the bat; and there is no run,
A handsome stroke to mid-off: and there is no run,
Brown brushes the next one away to mid-wicket; and there is no run,
He drives the last ball but fails to find the gap; and there is no run.
Zzzz.

EDDIE THOMPSON

JENNY'S DRONES

With tape-recorder, nail scissors, hearing aid and glasses,
I've gone along for ten years now to Jenny's fiddle classes

There we learn, by ear, mazurkas, reels and jigs,
Then play them at weddings, folk festivals and gigs.

I know that I'm not good enough to busk along The Strand,
But that doesn't bother me, 'cos now I'm in the band.

There I'm given one note, to cherish as my own,
I'm a "Poor Johnny One Note" - yes, I'm a drone.

I'm not on my own mind; I'm not quite a loner,
There's Wendy and me, and sometimes Fiona.

Whatever note I'm given, I play it loud and strong,
And, it has to be said, occasionally wrong.

I place my bow upon the strings and adopt an upright stance,
Then I worry and I wait for our long-awaited chance.

Some play the harmony, others play the tune,
We play just one note - invariably too soon.

Now that I'm established, as a regular drone,
I'm spending many hours indoors, sitting by the phone.

I've only one regret; I suppose it's quite absurd,
My "Twinkle Twinkle Little Star" will never now be heard.

March '05

THE FATE OF POETS

It isn't their moving poetry so much,
It's their interesting private lives
Their need for a psychological crutch,
Their interesting lovers and wives
But biography puts the poet on trial,
Unfairly after they're dead,
Usually the poets' lives they defile,
Leaving their poetry mainly unread.
So I would like to read of the skeletons discovered,
In the dark corners of Wendy Cope's cupboard.

SO WHY DO I DO IT?

I'm just not man enough,
To sing Rachmaninoff
His Vespers at least
I regard as a beast
And in Russian to boot,
It's an absolute brute
The second bass line is so low and so boring,
Whilst other voices have lines that go soaring
I'm there in a fog,
An impenetrable bog,
So why do I do it
When I should say screw it?
Who knows?
But here goes.

COCK ROBIN IS ALIVE AND WELL

Yesterday, when wondering what the day had in store
We witnessed a wooing outside our back door,
A pair of robin redbreasts,
In their clearly visible red vests,
Stood facing each other, just inches apart,
And danced a display that tugged at the heart
Both of them swayed from side to side,
The avian version of the Palais Glide
"Stick with me babe", he seemed to be saying,
Serious stuff he wasn't playing
Reaching and stretching a high as he could.
She seemed impressed and nodded she would,
For privacy they hopped out of view,
He'd pulled with his well-oiled, well-honed woo.

ACCENTS (2)

Accents
Are, to all intents,
A labelling
Enabling
Others to identify your clan,
Your source, where your voyage began
They speak of variations,
Of lost historic nations.

A tribe, by speech, is unified,
Instilling solidarity, identity and pride,
RP (Received Pronunciation)
Is clear, concise, but denies location,
So may regional accents flourish and thrive
Allowing our patchwork quilt to survive.
As for losing an accent to make your way,
That's far too high a price to pay.

PLACE

I've got this thing about place, where you were born and bred,
It's not that I'm being nosey; I can't get it out of my head
On meeting someone initially, I immediately set out to trace
Their place of birth, their origin, their maybe sacred space.

This interest stems from a discredited theory,
An old idea that makes geographers weary
That place determines attitude,
A theory that granted too much latitude.

It's more than just an ice-breaker, though that's how it must sound
It's a grudging belief in the theory and a search for common ground
We're a weave of many factors, a unique and intricate lace,
And though you may disagree, an important ingredient, is place.

LIFE'S STEEPLECHASE

So where am I in life's steeplechase?
Never a favourite, never a place
An also-ran to make up the card,
Dangerously close to the knacker's yard
A rank outsider, still gamely running,
Just clearing the jumps, nothing stunning
But slow and steady could win the race,
In this topsy-turvy steeplechase.

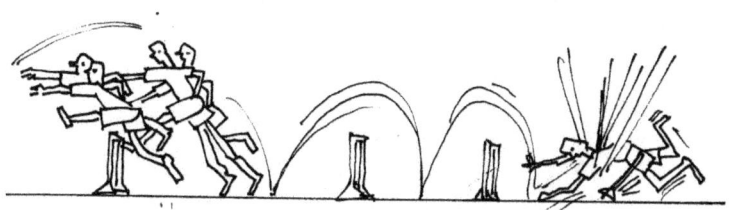

HYPE

"This book will change your life",
But that isn't the case, ask my wife
It's page after page of perfectly pure
Horse manure.
"You'll see this book as a catalyst"
Who penned those words must have been pissed
It may change the life of the person who wrote it,
Providing it sells, hence the hype to float it
"This book will change your life?"
Well I'm waiting, and so is my wife.

KEEPING CALM

It's my social drug of choice, and perfectly legit,
And well within my budget, at a few pence per hit
It induces in the wild a relaxed carefree calm,
Eases our anxieties, so really, where's the harm?
An altered state of consciousness? No, not quite, not really
But if taken off the market, I would miss it, clearly.
It's not yet allocated to class A, B or C,
So indulge before it is - ask for camomile tea.

A DEFENCE MECHANISM?

What is it with these positive thinkers?
Why do they spend so much time wearing blinkers?
Why would they want to deny reality?
Why the annoying false joviality?
Is it a sort of inner defence?
That constant smile, that blatant pretence?
Eventually it's wearisome, strange though that may sound
Why can't they find the balance? It's there to be found.

WELCOME TO LITTER WORLD

Welcome to litter world
Please be upstanding whilst our flag's unfurled
Ah, you're surprised! It's a damp-stained old curtain,
Rescued from a rubbish pile, of that you can be certain
It's symbolic of our state,
Trash is now a national trait
We're a race of litter bugs, litter reigns supreme
Of environmental vandals, we're the tops, we're the cream.

BREAKING WIND IN CHAPEL

Breaking wind in Chapel was an act of naked aggression,
Release required no effort other than inner compression,
It would wend its way along the seat of the ancient pitch pine pew,
To escape and explode in the open, that, we knew, was our cue
We would turn to our innocent neighbour, with a look of pure disgust,
Which condemned the poor unfortunate, and was totally unjust
But the minister knew better, even though partially deaf
"Nice note lads" he'd say, "a B in the key of C major, if you use the bass clef."

CULTURE? WHOSE CULTURE?

Quiet please! Right, Mozart's Requiem, you'll all know this
What do you mean, I'm taking the piss?
Surely you know the Lacrimosa?
No I'm not, I'm not a poser.
I know you're not ex choirboys,
And no, it isn't just a noise
Look, this is a pub, where do you think you are?
In a bloody conservatoire?
All right, all right, don't get into a strop,
Emrys, Delilah, from the top.

THE VISIT

On our front lawn (I use the term loosely),
Something strange has appeared, and it's growing profusely
It's a perfect circle, six feet wide,
With tiny toadstools tucked inside
It's a fairy circle and no mistake,
And you have my word, it's not a fake
Neither palaces nor ivory towers,
Of all the places, they've chosen ours.
I shall say hello as I go by,
And yes, I can hear your scornful sigh
If you think I've 'lost it' don't you grieve,
For I am Manx, and the Manx believe.

A SORT-OF CONVERSATION

We're Manx,
No, not Yanks,
Watch my lips, M-A-N-X, Manx.
From the Isle of Man,
No, I didn't say I love Bran,
Is your hearing aid switched on?
In the Irish Sea,
Irish, Irish, not Sky Dish,
But I AM pronouncing my consonants.
It's a Crown Dependency,
No, no one drowned in the deep end,
Is the battery flat?
We have three legs on our emblem,
EMBLEM! EMBLEM! Not PENDULUM!
I AM NOT GETTING CROSS!
All right, OK, our cats have no tails
Who's talking about hats in the sales?
Hell's teeth! You're not even trying.
You may have heard of Manx kippers?
No, no, no, not prank strippers!
That's it, I'm off.

THE POST

The mail has arrived and I meander to the door,
Wearing a sort of smile
I cast my eyes on the postal pile,
Scattered on the floor.

But anticipation isn't there, compared with years gone by
When correspondence
Cleared despondence.
Now it's 'junk mail', and I heave a sigh.

Yet hope springs eternal that this might be the day,
That something arrives
To lift our lives
In some significant way.

It doesn't look promising, I have to admit,
A magazine for Sky TV,
Bumf for an arthritic knee,
Nothing to appeal to an old sad git.

There's a catalogue, the water bill, something meant for 37,
I've won 10,000 euros again,
Cash required for Wicken Fen,
Holidays in sunny Devon

Bribes to switch my car insurance, credit card and gas provider,
A lengthy questionnaire,
A miraculous cure for thinning hair,
Reader's Digest, spreading knowledge ever wider.

Sifting the pile with my foot, morale takes a turn for the better
This envelope looks inviting
With a stamp and exceedingly neat handwriting,
Can it be? Yes it is, great Scott - a letter!

RED TAPED

I'm fed up to the teeth with Terms and Conditions
And Rules and Regulations on, say, carbon emissions
With living on a diet of Important Information
Truly I have reached a point of saturation
Agreements, Directions, Notes for Completing
Ubiquitous Instructions constantly bleating
Statements, Reviews and At a Glance Guides
Have put me in a rut, with extremely high sides
Codes, Summaries and Schedules they really take the biscuit
So, to shred or not to shred? Will I ever risk it?

OH NO! A BASS ENTRY!

We're on our feet
Counting the beat.

The others are wary,
Bass entries are scary.

A clearing of throats
A selection of notes.

A hint of panic,
Nothing manic.

This is it,
The fuse is lit.

We come in strong -
We come in wrong.

"AND WE SHALL BE CHANGED"

So what was it that changed your life's course?
Do you see it as fate, that mysterious force?

Can you recall the intersection,
The point at which you changed direction?

Was it a book, an event, a woman or man?
Or did your life go according to plan?

Or was alcohol the catalyst?
Were you, maybe, Brahms and Liszt?

If there was a plan, who plotted the chart?
And who or what prised you apart?

Did you decide, as quick as a blink.
Without ever stopping to think?

To the despair of others,
(Especially mothers)

Who viewed your deviation
With utter consternation

Your course was changed,
Your life rearranged

But a life devoid of twists and turns,
Is a life light on experience, a life that never learns.

LONGER ONES

Verses in this genre are longer than a page,
Thankfully few ever reach this stage.

Fortuna, Goddess of Luck
Sound Memories
Second Basses
The History Lesson

FORTUNA, GODDESS OF LUCK

O Fortuna, Goddess of Luck,
Where did you stand in the Roman pantheon of gods?
You weren't a Premier League player,
You weren't up there with Venus, Diana or Minerva
But as the daughter of Jupiter
You were destined to be a player,
You were there, in the ruck.

O Fortuna, Goddess of Luck,
Were you subjected to the biological upheavals
Experienced by mere mortal females?
Were you then easily offended?
Did you then scatter only bad luck?
Did your followers know to keep low?
Was it time to duck?

O Fortuna, Goddess of Luck,
Blindly dispensing both good and bad fortune,
A wheel flies off a chariot just twenty cubits from the finish.
Bad luck?
No, somehow the charioteer had offended Fortuna,
Maybe he had served in Jerusalem,
Maybe he called her a schmuck.

O Fortuna, Goddess of Luck,
What of your worshippers now?
Their pilgrimage sites include Aintree, Epsom and Redcar,
Your altars are in betting shops and casinos,
Your priests are bookmakers and croupiers,
And your followers are punters
Your honour is being dragged through the muck

But O Fortuna, Goddess of Luck,
Take heart, for you are not completely debased
Shakespeare honours you with a mention in his Sonnet 29,
Carl Orff too in his Carmina Burana
And there's Frankie Laine's hit, 'O Wheel of Fortune', in the 1950s
You are still seen by some to be steering us,
Capricious though you may be,
And your followers will return your smile and bless you,
When things go well and they make a quick buck.

SOUND MEMORIES

Certain memories rekindle a life,
A life led long ago
For me it's the sound of a prop-driven aircraft,
Flying fairly low
It sends me back to the early fifties,
A difficult time we know,
When I was fifteen, sixteen, seventeen,
And my life seemed painfully slow.

I'm sitting on the summit,
Of a cool North Barrule,
Looking out beyond the sea,
A sea that is always cruel
And I can 'see' the hills of Galloway,
As the drone my memories fuel
And I was old enough to realize
That the Island is a jewel.

I can 'see' hotels on Ramsey's prom,
Tall, straight, dressed off by the right,
Holding holidaymakers
With the season at its height
Then internees, caged behind barbed wire
Once totally unaware that this would be their plight,
And Jurby church, and the lighthouse on the Point,
Both glistening in the sun, a shining bright gloss white.

Ted, our cocker spaniel, is panting by my side,
My ever-faithful four-legged friend
A plane flies by beneath us, maybe from Blackpool to Belfast,
If so, it's half way to its journey's end.
There's a strong feeling of oneness with what I can 'see' below,
It's a lovely, natural, mystical blend
So there you have it, my special sound, a piston-engined aircraft
It makes me stop and listen, and to my memory attend.

SECOND BASSES

My life among the second basses
Is not all beer and whisky chasers
For in amongst those puzzled faces,
Dwell several really lurid cases.

Groping round the lower reaches,
Frowned upon by music teachers,
Shunned by several first bass preachers,
We nonetheless boast several features

EDDIE THOMPSON

For example, steeped in art,
Painter Peter sees his part
As passing wind before we start.
To which we pitch with eager heart

And that Elizabethan gent,
Knightly Randolph, kind, well meant
Whatever was his high intent?
His voice an octave lower went.

And "Little John", arriving late,
Redeems himself, as is his trait,
By crashing in through every gate
Two beats early, sure as fate.

May Ray and John and Robin too
And others in that gallant few
Still try their hand to quietly woo
The soloist on hire from Kew.

May second basses shine for thee,
May second basses sing in key
Please, not another Mass in C,
Please God, a simple one for me.

Second basses, second basses,
Clear your throats and take your places
Lift the roof and kick the traces,
Oh you lovely second basses.

THE HISTORY LESSON

A little rhyme may help to prime
You in examinations
You could do worse, I do believe
Than have a verse tucked up your sleeve.

Hang it on your memory bank,
Unhook it should your mind go blank
Use it to disperse blue fogs,
Use it to lubricate the cogs.

In ten sixty-six came that Norman invader,
Slayer of Saxons, tyrant, dictator,
William the Conqueror, William the First,
'William the Bastard', William the cursed.

At a quarter past twelve
King John did barter
His life and crown
For the Magna Carta.

EDDIE THOMPSON

Flayer and deceiver of Celts
For conquest an insatiable thirst
That bloody, vicious Plantagenet,
Warmonger Edward the First.

Gay, unwarlike, most unkingly,
But who would have reckoned
On his murderous end?
Skewered, Edward the Second.

Much maligned by Shakespeare,
And since has been given the bird,
And those two princes in the Tower?
Guilty bastard, Richard the Third.

Founder of the Church of England,
Defender of the Faith,
That 'syphilitic sleazeball*'
Henery the Eighth.

Cruel, mean
Decidedly scary
That Tudor terror,
'Bloody Mary'.

Wooed by many, won by none,
Though it's said that Essex came close
Good Queen Bess, Elizabeth the First
Whose gallant little fleet Phillip's bubble burst.

POETRY LITE

He was Sixth then First,
And survived the Gunpowder Plot,
To whom do I refer?
King James, the ginger Scot.

With the death of the Lord Protector
The Puritan's Taleban got the sack
So let's hear it for Charles the Second,
Christmas and partying were back.

It's the Empress of India,
'Midst imperial euphoria
So cover up the piano legs,
Here comes Queen Victoria.

Lille Langtry, the 'Jersey Lily',
Was steered (willingly) bedward
By the randy, eponymous
Seventh King Edward.

Fixated,
Abdicated,
Segregated,
Edward the Eighth.

The above are just examples
To give you the general idea,
Of course it may not work for you
If it does, you owe me a beer.

A descriptive phrase for Henry VIII in The Times, late August '09. Copy lost, author unknown.

www.ingramcontent.com/pod-product-compliance
Lightning Source LLC
Chambersburg PA
CBHW061339040426
42444CB00011B/3003